HAL•LEONARD

ESSENTIAL SONGS

PIANO VOCAL GUITAR

Love Songs

ISBN 0-634-08047-4

HAL•LEONARD®
CORPORATION

7777 W. BLUEMOUND RD. P.O. BOX 13819 MILWAUKEE, WI 53213

Visit Hal Leonard Online at
www.halleonard.com

CONTENTS

ALL FOR LOVE
from Walt Disney Pictures' THE THREE MUSKETEERS

Words and Music by BRYAN ADAMS,
ROBERT LANGE and MICHAEL KAMEN

ALL I ASK OF YOU
from THE PHANTOM OF THE OPERA

Music by ANDREW LLOYD WEBBER
Lyrics by CHARLES HART
Additional Lyrics by RICHARD STILGOE

No more talk of dark - ness, for - get these wide - eyed fears: I'm

here, noth - ing can harm you, my words will warm and calm you.

Let me be your free - dom, let day - light dry your tears: I'm

ALL OUT OF LOVE

Words and Music by GRAHAM RUSSELL
and CLIVE DAVIS

I'm ly-ing a-lone _ with my head on the phone _
want you to come _ back and car-ry me home _ a-

think-ing of you _ 'til it hurts. _
way from these long _ lone-ly nights. _
I know you hurt, too, _ but what
I'm reach-ing for you. _ Are you

ALL MY LOVING

Words and Music by JOHN LENNON
and PAUL McCARTNEY

you, _____ all ___ my lov-ing, ___ dar-

- ling, I'll ___ be true. _____

ALMOST PARADISE

Love Theme from the Paramount Motion Picture FOOTLOOSE

Words by DEAN PITCHFORD
Music by ERIC CARMEN

ALWAYS ON MY MIND

Words and Music by WAYNE THOMPSON,
MARK JAMES and JOHNNY CHRISTOPHER

BABY, I LOVE YOUR WAY

Words and Music by
PETER FRAMPTON

AMANDA

Words and Music by
TOM SCHOLZ

Babe, to-mor-row's so far a-way. There's some-thin' I just have to say.

I don't think I could hide what I'm feel-in' in-side an-

You and I,___ I know that we___ can't wait.___ And I swear,___ I swear it's not a lie,___ girl. To-mor-row may be too late.___

AND I LOVE HER

Words and Music by JOHN LENNON
and PAUL McCARTNEY

Lyrics:

I give her all my love, _____ that's all I do. _____
She gives me ev - 'ry - thing _____ and ten - der - ly. _____
Bright are the stars _____ that shine, _____ dark is the sky. _____

End instrumental solo

And I love ___

___ her. ___

BACK AT ONE

Words and Music by
BRIAN McKNIGHT

CAN'T WE TRY

Words and Music by DAN HILL
Additional Lyrics by BEVERLY CHAPIN-HILL

Moderately slow

Am7

(He:) I see your face cloud o - ver like a lit - tle girl's___ and your eyes___
hear you on the tel - e - phone with God knows who

G(add9)

___ spill - ing out your lost heart have lost their shine.___ their for free.___ You

F(add9)

whis - per some - thing soft - ly I'm not meant to hear. Ba - by,
Ev - 'ry - one has some - one they___ can talk to.

BEST OF MY LOVE

Words and Music by MAURICE WHITE
and AL McKAY

With moderate movement

Does-n't take ___ much to make ___ me ___ hap - py ___ and make ___ me ___ smile ___ with glee. ___

Nev - er, nev - er will I feel ___ dis - cour - aged ___ 'cause our love's ___ no mys - ter - y. ___

BREATHE

Words and Music by HOLLY LAMAR
and STEPHANIE BENTLEY

Moderately fast

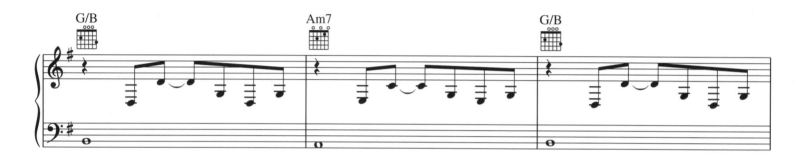

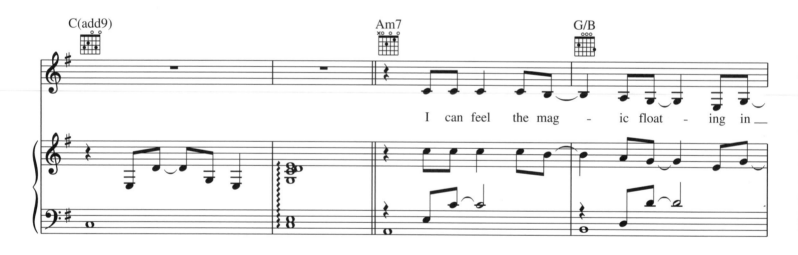

I can feel the mag - ic float - ing in ___

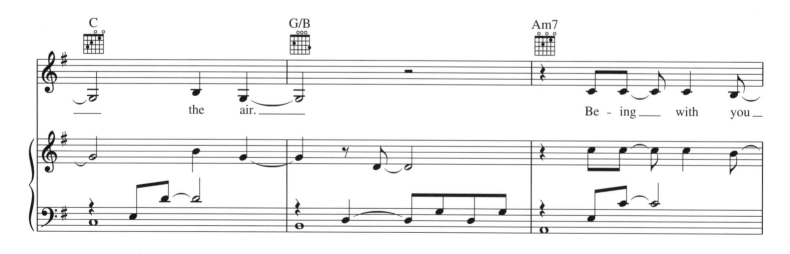

the air. ___ Be - ing ___ with you ___

Can You Feel The Love Tonight

from Walt Disney Pictures' THE LION KING

Music by ELTON JOHN
Lyrics by TIM RICE

Pop Ballad

mp legato

With pedal

There's a calm ___ sur-ren - der
There's a time ___ for ev-'ry-one,

to the rush ___ of day, ___ when the heat ___ of the roll-ing world ___
if they on - ly learn ___ that the twist - ing ka-lei-do-scope ___

can be turned ___ a - way. ___ An en-chant-ed mo-ment,
moves us all ___ in turn. ___ There's a rhyme ___ and rea - son

CAN'T HELP FALLING IN LOVE

Words and Music by GEORGE DAVID WEISS,
HUGO PERETTI and LUIGI CREATORE

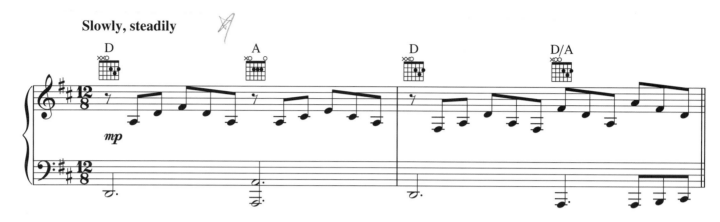

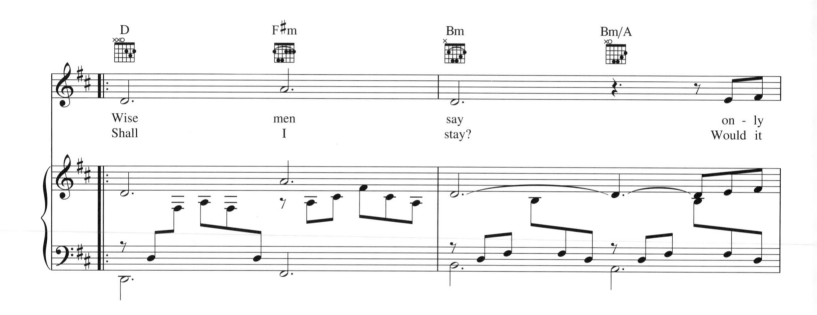

Wise   men   say   on - ly
Shall   I   stay?   Would it

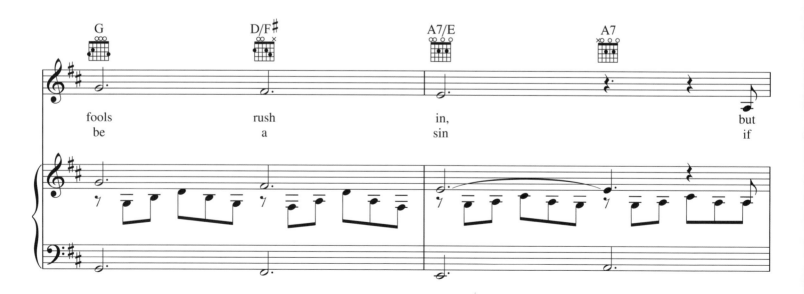

fools   rush   in,   but
be   a   sin   if

THE COLOUR OF LOVE

Words and Music by BILLY OCEAN,
JOLYON SKINNER, BARRY EASTMAN
and WAYNE BRATHWAITE

B
D♯m7
C♯m
E/F♯
What is the col - our of love?
What do you see?
true.
G♯m
D♯m7
C♯m
E/F♯
Is it warm, is it ten - der when you think of me?
B
D♯m7
C♯m7
E/F♯
I see the col - our of love when I'm think - ing of you
E
B/D♯
C♯7
E/F♯
Repeat ad lib. and Fade
as a pic - ture per - fect paint - ing of love for - ev - er

COULD I HAVE THIS DANCE

Words and Music by WAYLAND HOLYFIELD
and BOB HOUSE

ENDLESS LOVE

Words and Music by
LIONEL RICHIE

Oh, _____ and _ love, _____

ETERNAL FLAME

Words and Music by BILLY STEINBERG,
TOM KELLY and SUSANNA HOFFS

*Recorded a half step lower.

THE FIRST TIME

Words and Music by BERNARD JACKSON
and BRIAN SIMPSON

You know I won't for-get ___ the times ___ we shared ___ to-geth-er hold-ing hands
Al-though some-time has passed, ___ I still ___ re-mem-ber just ___ like it was yes-

THE FIRST TIME EVER I SAW YOUR FACE

Words and Music by
EWAN MacCOLL

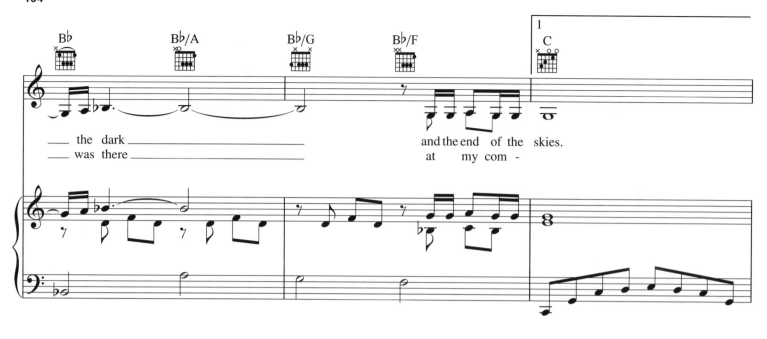

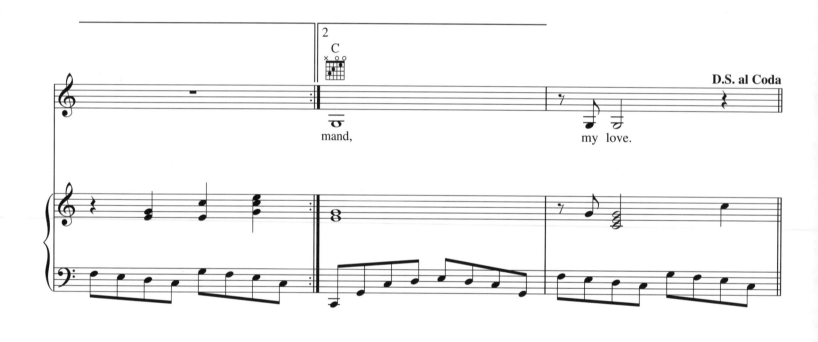

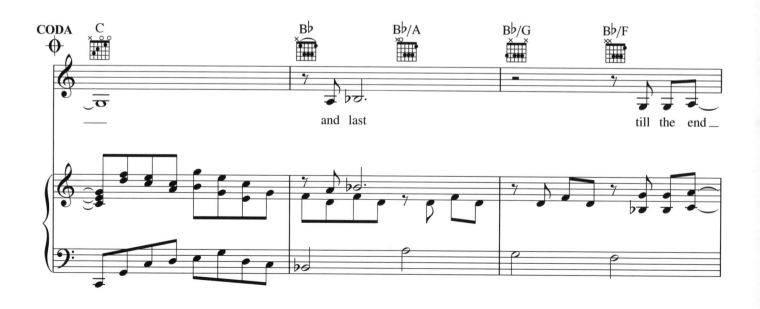

FOR THE FIRST TIME

Words and Music by JAMES NEWTON HOWARD,
JUD FRIEDMAN and ALLAN RICH

Moderately slow

FROM THIS MOMENT ON

Words and Music by SHANIA TWAIN
and R.J. LANGE

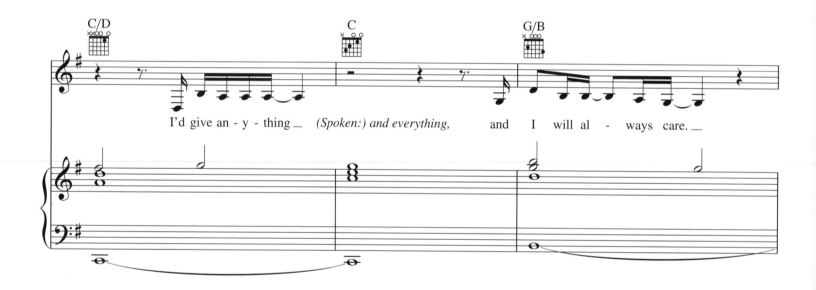

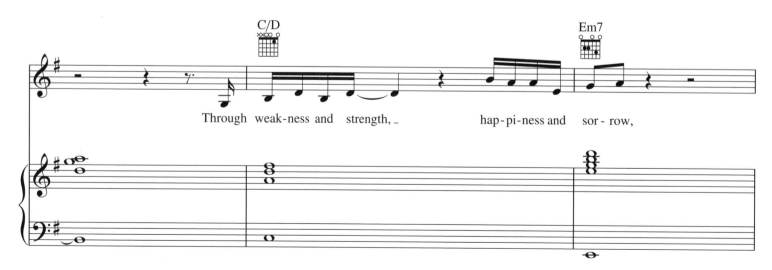

*Male vocals sung an octave higher throughout.

prom-ise you this. _____ There is noth - ing I would-n't give, _____

from this mo-ment on. ____

Female: You're the rea - son I ___ be - lieve ___ in love, _____

Male: and you're the an - swer to ___ my prayers ___ from

HAVE I TOLD YOU LATELY

Words and Music by
VAN MORRISON

Have I told ___ you late-ly that I love you? Have I

told you there's no one else ___ a-bove ___ you?

Fill my heart ___ with glad-ness, take a-way all ___ my sad-ness,

GLORY OF LOVE
Theme from KARATE KID PART II

Words and Music by DAVID FOSTER,
PETER CETERA and DIANE NINI

HERE AND NOW

Words and Music by TERRY STEELE
and DAVID ELLIOT

HOW AM I SUPPOSED TO LIVE WITHOUT YOU

Words and Music by MICHAEL BOLTON
and DOUG JAMES

HOW DEEP IS YOUR LOVE

from the Motion Picture SATURDAY NIGHT FEVER

Words and Music by ROBIN GIBB,
MAURICE GIBB and BARRY GIBB

I CAN'T STOP LOVING YOU

Words and Music by
DON GIBSON

Those hap-py hours _____ that we once knew, _____ though long a - go, _____ still make me blue. _____ They say that

I FINALLY FOUND SOMEONE
from THE MIRROR HAS TWO FACES

Words and Music by BARBRA STREISAND,
MARVIN HAMLISCH, ROBERT LANGE and BRYAN ADAMS

Male: I fi-n'lly found some-one who knocks me off my feet.

I fi-n'lly found the one __ that makes me feel com-plete.

Female: It start-ed o-ver cof-fee. We start-ed out as friends.

I HONESTLY LOVE YOU

Words and Music by PETER ALLEN
and JEFF BARRY

Maybe I hang a-round__ here a lit-tle more than I should; we
You don't__ have to an - swer; I see it in your eyes.

both know I got some - where else __ to go. But
May-be it was bet - ter left __ un-said. But

I JUST CALLED TO SAY I LOVE YOU

Words and Music by
STEVIE WONDER

Additional Lyrics

3. No summer's high; no warm July;
   No harvest moon to light one tender August night.
   No autumn breeze; no falling leaves;
   Not even time for birds to fly to southern skies.

4. No Libra sun; no Halloween;
   No giving thanks to all the Christmas joy you bring.
   But what it is, though old so new
   To fill your heart like no three words could ever do.
   Chorus

I THINK I LOVE YOU
featured in the Television Series THE PARTRIDGE FAMILY

Words and Music by
TONY ROMEO

I WILL REMEMBER YOU
Theme from THE BROTHERS McMULLEN

Words and Music by SARAH McLACHLAN,
SEAMUS EGAN and DAVE MERENDA

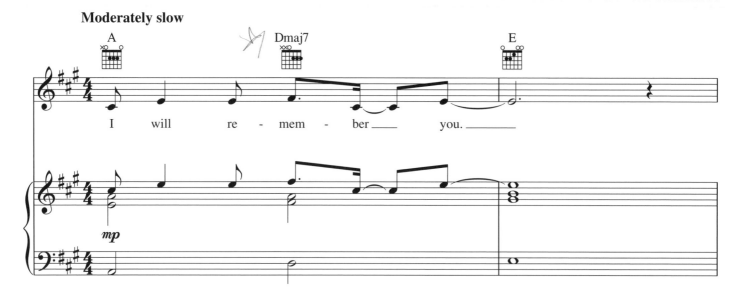

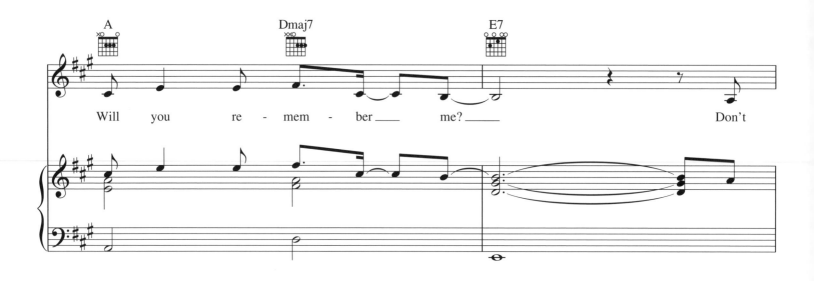

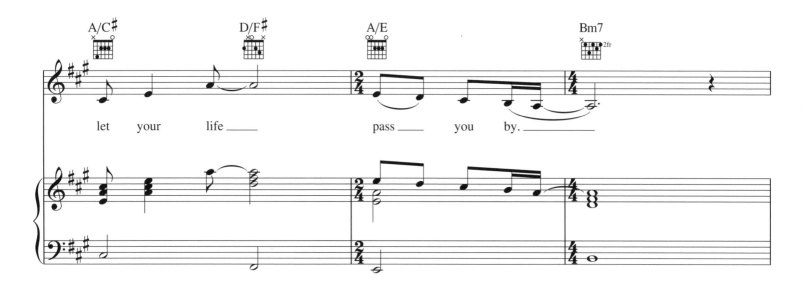

I'LL BE THERE

Words and Music by BERRY GORDY,
HAL DAVIS, WILLIE HUTCH and BOB WEST

I'LL BE

Words and Music by
EDWIN McCAIN

Recorded a half step lower.

I'LL BE THERE FOR YOU

Words and Music by JON BON JOVI
and RICHIE SAMBORA

I'LL HAVE TO SAY I LOVE YOU IN A SONG

Words and Music by
JIM CROCE

I'LL MAKE LOVE TO YOU

Words and Music by
BABYFACE

Close your eyes,   make a wish,   and blow
lax,   let's go wish slow.   I ain't

IF YOU LEAVE ME NOW

Words and Music by
PETER CETERA

- row comes, ___ then we'll both ___ re - gret ___ the things we said ___ to - day. ___

Ooh, _____ girl, _____ just
Ooh, ma - ma, _____ I just

got to have _ you by my side. _____
got to have _ your lov - in'. _____

Repeat and Fade

Ooh, _____

IT MUST HAVE BEEN LOVE

Words and Music by
PER GESSLE

JUST THE WAY YOU ARE

Words and Music by
BILLY JOEL

Gm   D/F#   Am7   D7   Gmaj7

- or of your hair. ___ Mm, _____ mm. _____ You al - ways

Gm6   D/F#   Bm7

have my _____ un - spok - en pas - sion, ___

E9sus   E9   A9sus

al - though I might ___ not seem to care. _____

D   Bm6   Gmaj7

___ I _____ don't _ want clev - er ___ con - ver -

KEEP ON LOVING YOU

Words and Music by
KEVIN CRONIN

LADY

Words and Music by
LIONEL RICHIE

LADY IN RED

Words and Music by
CHRIS DeBURGH

LET IT BE ME
(Je T'appartiens)

English Words by MANN CURTIS
French Words by PIERRE DeLANOE
Music by GILBERT BECAUD

LET'S GET IT ON

Words and Music by MARVIN GAYE
and ED TOWNSEND

Slow Soul beat

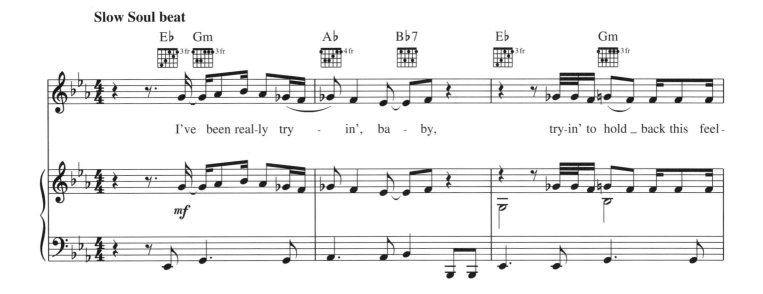

I've been real-ly try - in', ba - by, try-in' to hold _ back this feel-

in' for so ___ long. And if you feel like _ I feel, _ ba-by,

then come on, _ on, ___ come on. Ooh, __ let's get it on. Ow, _____

LET THE RIVER RUN

Theme from the Motion Picture WORKING GIRL

Words and Music by
CARLY SIMON

LET'S STAY TOGETHER

Words and Music by AL GREEN,
WILLIE MITCHELL and AL JACKSON, JR.

LONGER

Words and Music by
DAN FOGELBERG

258

LOVE ME TENDER

Words and Music by ELVIS PRESLEY
and VERA MATSON

Moderately slow

Love me ten - der, love me sweet,
Love me ten - der, love me long,
Love me ten - der, love me dear,
When at last my dreams come true,

nev - er let me go.
take me to your heart,
tell me you are mine.
dar - ling, this I know:

You have made my
for it's there that
I'll be yours through
Hap - pi - ness will

LOVE TAKES TIME

Words and Music by MARIAH CAREY
and BEN MARGULIES

LOVE WILL KEEP US TOGETHER

Words and Music by NEIL SEDAKA
and HOWARD GREENFIELD

MANDY

Words and Music by SCOTT ENGLISH
and RICHARD KERR

LOVING YOU

Words and Music by JERRY LEIBER
and MIKE STOLLER

* Even eighth notes

MAYBE I'M AMAZED

Words and Music by
PAUL McCARTNEY

MY LOVE

Words and Music by
PAUL and LINDA McCARTNEY

Slowly, sensitively

And when I go a - way___ I know my heart can stay___ with my
And when the cup - board's bare___ I'll still find some - thing there___ with my
Don't ev - er ask me why___ I nev - er say good - bye___ to my

love. It's un - der - stood _____ It's in the hands_ of my love, _____
love. It's un - der - stood _____ It's ev - 'ry - where_ with my love, _____ and
love. It's un - der - stood _____ It's ev - 'ry - where_ with my love, _____

my love does it good, Wo wo wo wo, wo wo

MORE THAN WORDS

Words and Music by NUNO BETTENCOURT
and GARY CHERONE

* Recorded a half step lower.

MY HEART WILL GO ON
(Love Theme from 'Titanic')
from the Paramount and Twentieth Century Fox Motion Picture TITANIC

Music by JAMES HORNER
Lyric by WILL JENNINGS

Lyrics:
Ev - 'ry night in my dreams I see you, I feel you, that is how I know you go on.

ON THE WINGS OF LOVE

Words and Music by JEFFREY OSBORNE
and PETER SCHLESS

and I'm yours __ ex - clu - sive - ly. ___ And right now ___ we live __ and

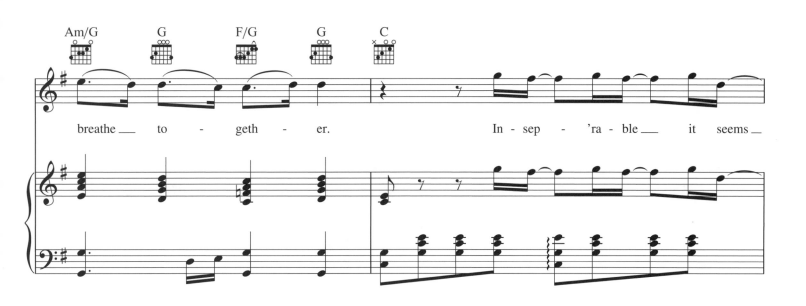

breathe __ to - geth - er. In - sep - 'ra - ble __ it seems __

__ we're flow - ing like __ a stream run - ning free trav - el - ing

PUT YOUR HEAD ON MY SHOULDER

Words and Music by
PAUL ANKA

Put your head on my shoul - der, hold me in your arms, ba - by. Squeeze me oh so tight, show me that you love me too. _____ Put your lips close to

SAVE THE BEST FOR LAST

Words and Music by PHIL GALDSTON,
JON LIND and WENDY WALDMAN

SEPARATE LIVES
Love Theme from WHITE NIGHTS

Words and Music by
STEPHEN BISHOP

Slowly, freely

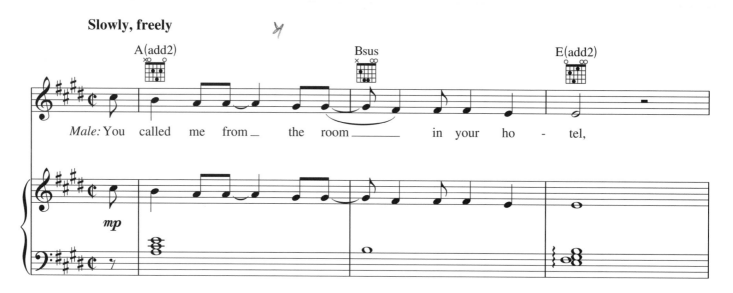

Male: You called me from the room in your ho- tel,

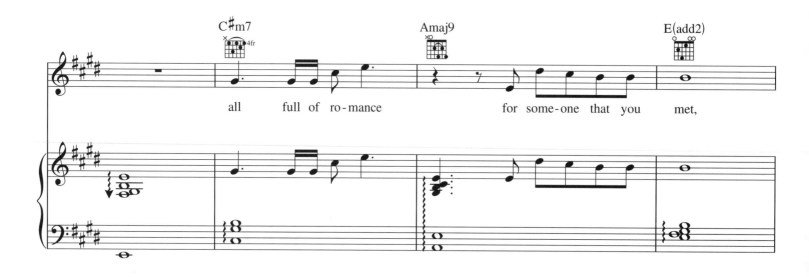

all full of ro- mance for some- one that you met,

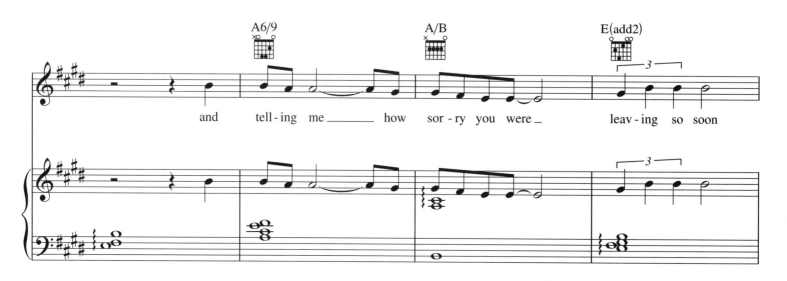

and tell- ing me how sor- ry you were leav- ing so soon

SEPTEMBER MORN

Words and Music by NEIL DIAMOND
and GILBERT BECAUD

SHE'S GOT A WAY
from MOVIN' OUT

Words and Music by
BILLY JOEL

SOMETHING

Words and Music by
GEORGE HARRISON

Some - thing in ___ the way ___ she moves,
Some - where in ___ her smile ___ she knows
Some - thing in ___ the way ___ she knows,

at - tracts ___ me like ___ no oth - er lov - er.
that I ___ don't need ___ no oth - er lov - er.
and all ___ I have ___ to do is think ___ of her.

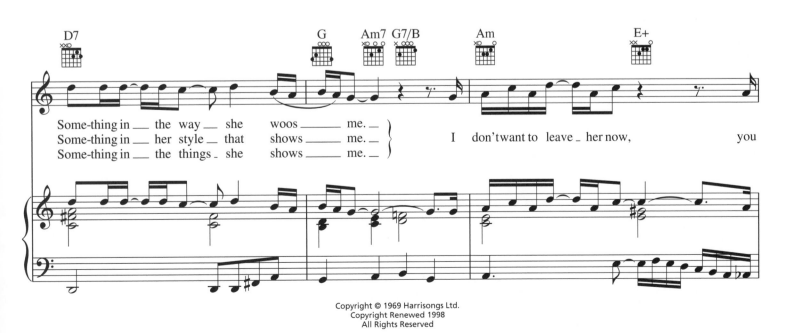

Some-thing in ___ the way ___ she woos ___ me. ___
Some-thing in ___ her style ___ that shows ___ me. ___
Some-thing in ___ the things ___ she shows ___ me. ___

I don't want to leave ___ her now, ___ you

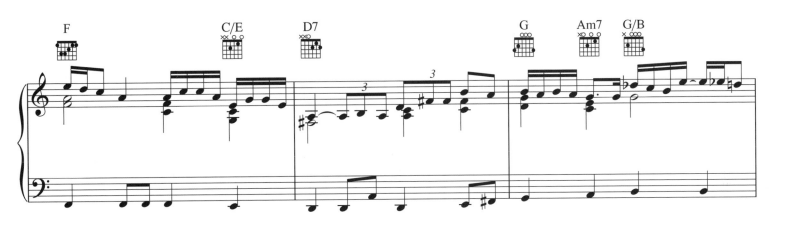

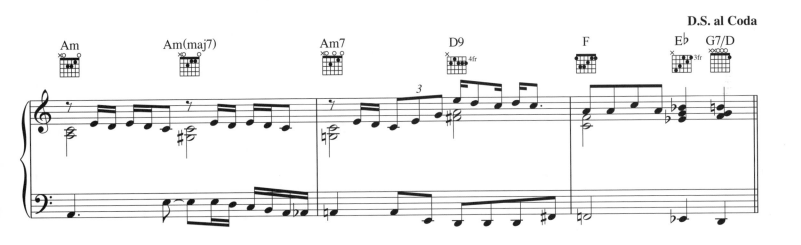

SOMEWHERE OUT THERE

from AN AMERICAN TAIL

Words and Music by JAMES HORNER,
BARRY MANN and CYNTHIA WEIL

through, then we'll be to-geth - er some-where out there, out

where dreams come true. _____

STRANGERS IN THE NIGHT
adapted from A MAN COULD GET KILLED

Words by CHARLES SINGLETON
and EDDIE SNYDER
Music by BERT KAEMPFERT

THREE TIMES A LADY

Words and Music by
LIONEL RICHIE

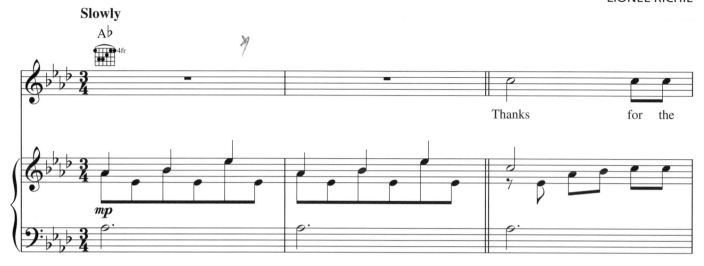

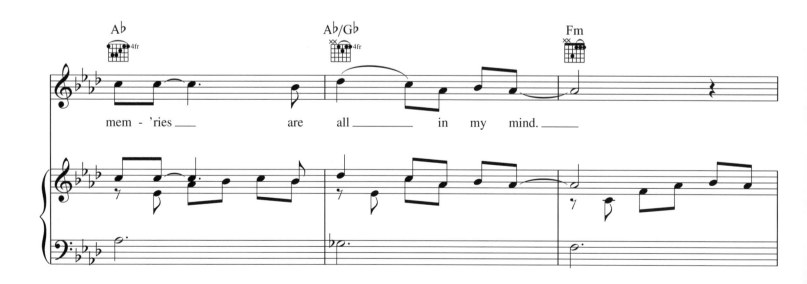

TIME AFTER TIME

Words and Music by CYNDI LAUPER
and ROB HYMAN

UNCHAINED MELODY
from the Motion Picture UNCHAINED

Lyric by HY ZARET
Music by ALEX NORTH

WE'VE ONLY JUST BEGUN

Words and Music by ROGER NICHOLS
and PAUL WILLIAMS

WHAT THE WORLD NEEDS NOW IS LOVE

Lyric by HAL DAVID
Music by BURT BACHARACH

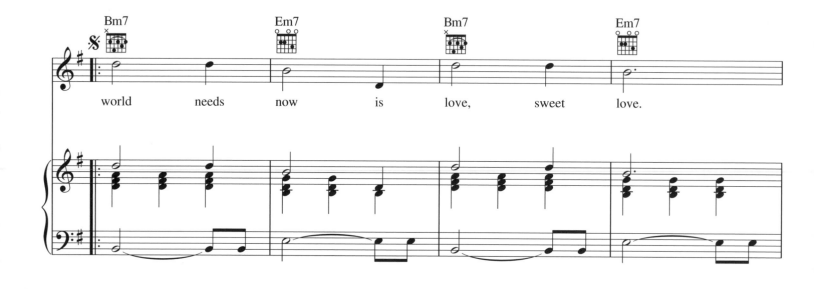

WOMAN

Words and Music by
JOHN LENNON

Moderately slow

WHERE DO I BEGIN
(Love Theme)
from the Paramount Picture LOVE STORY

Words by CARL SIGMAN
Music by FRANCIS LAI

love that an-y-where I go _____ I'm nev-er

lone-ly. _____ With her a-long, _____ who could be

lone-ly? _____ I reach for her hand; _____ it's al-ways there. _____

__ How long does it last? _____ Can love be meas-ured by the

WONDERFUL TONIGHT

Words and Music by
ERIC CLAPTON

Moderately

It's late in the eve - ning;
We go to a par - ty,
It's time to go home ___ now,

she's won-d'ring what clothes ___ to wear. ___
and ev - 'ry - one turns ___ to see ___
and I've got an ach - ing head. ___

She puts on her make -
this beau - ti - ful la -
So I give her the car

YOU ARE MY LADY

Words and Music by
BARRY EASTMAN

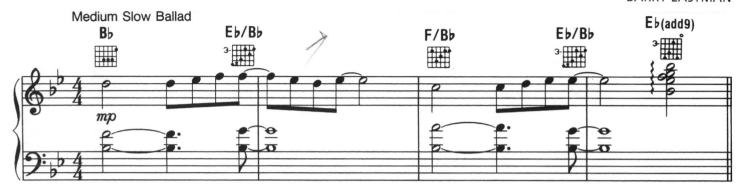

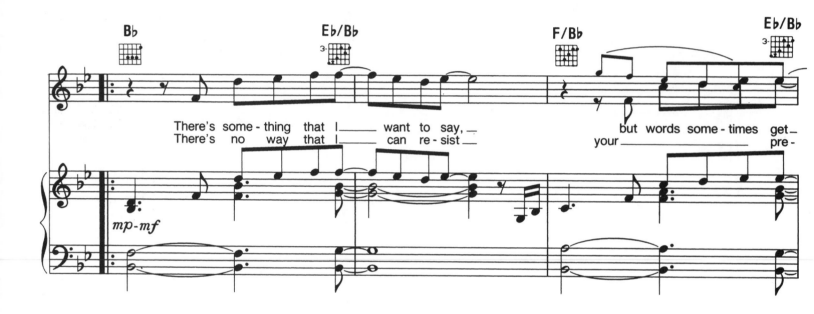

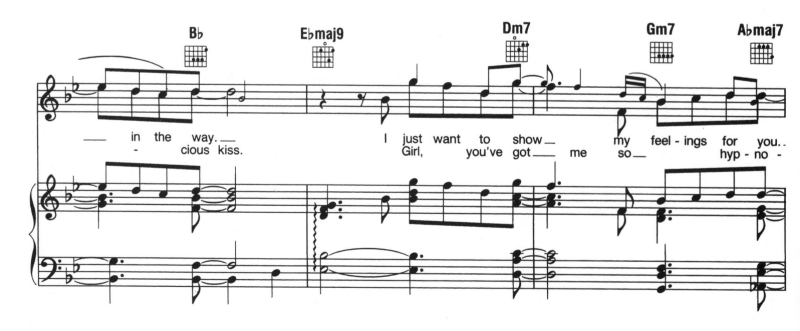

YOU ARE SO BEAUTIFUL

Words and Music by BILLY PRESTON
and BRUCE FISHER

Moderately slow, expressively

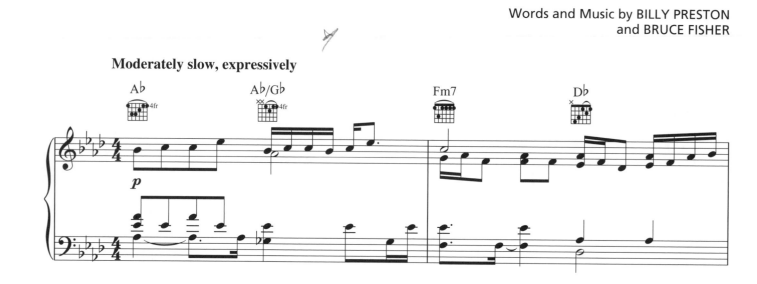

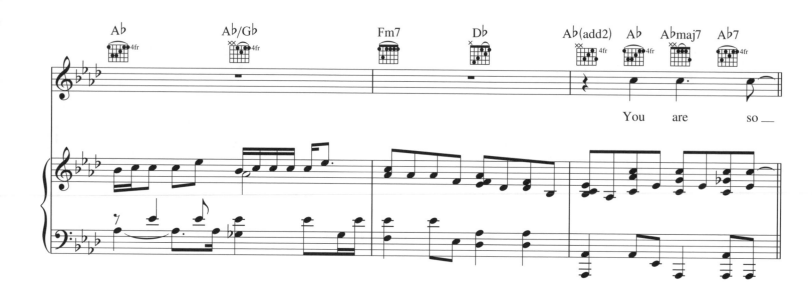

You are so __

__ beau - ti - ful __

to

8vb   *loco*

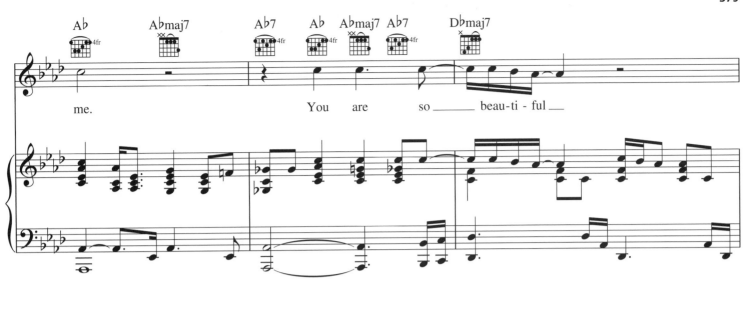

hope for.
hope for,

You're _ ev -'ry - thing I need. _

You are so _ beau-ti - ful _ to me. _

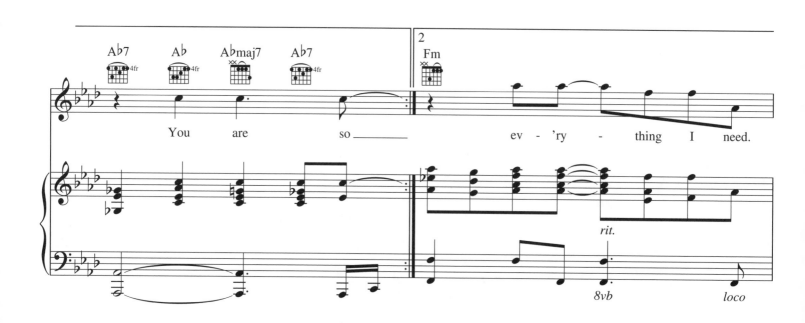

You are so _ ev - 'ry - thing I need.

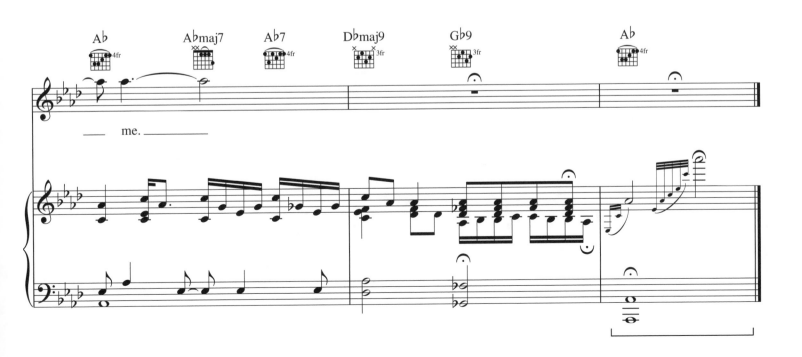

YOU LIGHT UP MY LIFE

Words and Music by
JOSEPH BROOKS

So man - y nights, I'd
Roll - in' at sea, a -

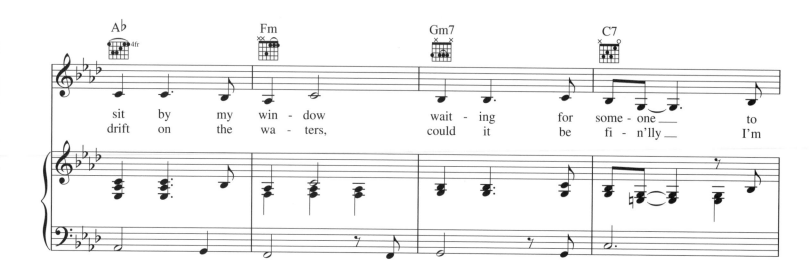

sit by my win - dow wait - ing for some - one ___ to
drift on the wa - ters, could it be fi - n'lly ___ I'm

sing me his song. So man - y dreams I
turn - ing for home? Fi - n'lly a chance to

YOU'RE STILL THE ONE

Words and Music by SHANIA TWAIN
and R.J. LANGE

Looks like we made ___ it. Look how far ___ we've come, ___ my ba - by. _____
Ain't noth - in' bet - ter, we beat ___ the odds ___ to - geth - er. _____

We might-a took the long ___ way. We knew ___ we'd get ___ there some - day. _____
I'm glad we did - n't lis - ten. Look at what we would ___ be miss - ing. _____

They said, "I bet ___ they'll nev - er make ___ it." But just

look at ___ us hold - ing ___ on. _____ We're still to - geth -

YOUR SONG

Words and Music by ELTON JOHN
and BERNIE TAUPIN

Lyrics:
now that it's done, _____ I hope you don't mind, _____ I hope you don't mind _____ that I put _____ down in words how won-der-ful life is _____ while you're _____ in _____ the world. _____

YOU'RE IN MY HEART

Words and Music by
ROD STEWART

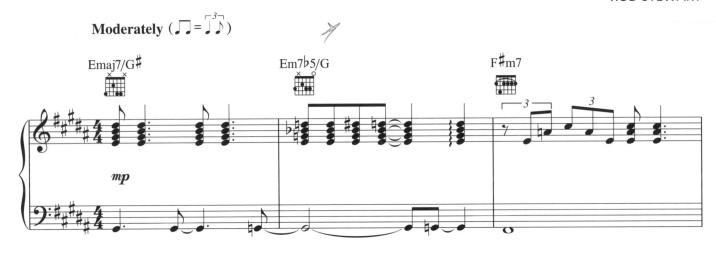

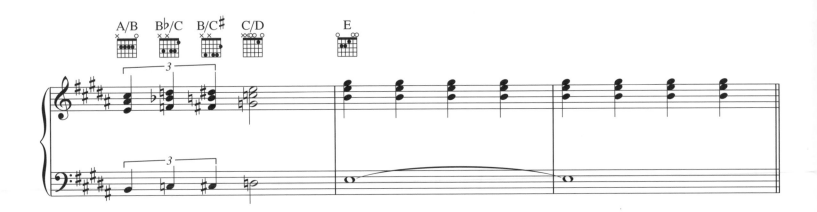

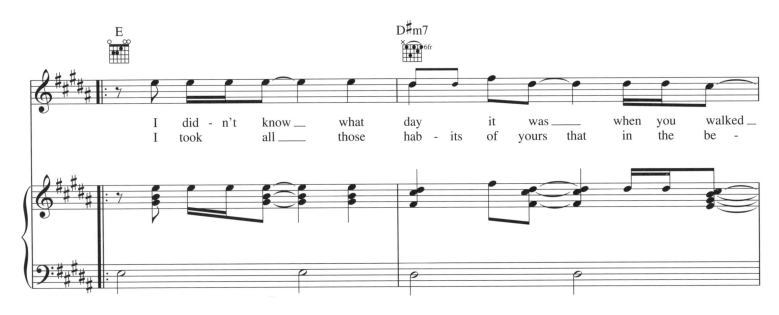

I did-n't know _ what day it was _ when you walked _
I took all _ those hab-its of yours that in the be -